Esse & Friends
Colouring and
Handwriting
Practice Workbook

Girl Friends

Colour us in!

Esse

NannaChar

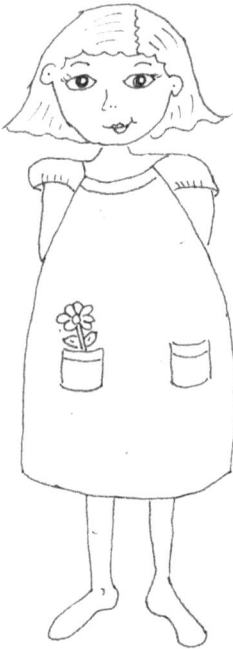

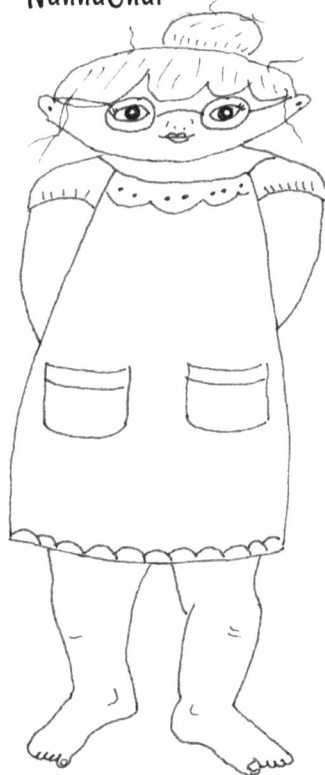

Esse & Friends Learning Books

Esse & Friends Colouring and Handwriting Practice WorkBook: Girl Friends
UK | Canadian | Austrralian Spelling

ISBN: 978-0-6486715-4-1

Also available in American Spelling and Hardcover versions.

Dearest Esse,

My darling grand-daughter; you may currently live on the other side of the world but you are always in my thoughts and heart.

Keep being gorgeous, kind, loving, forgiving, fair-minded, honest and curious.

Love it when we get to video chat. Love you always!

Bear hugs and sloppy kisses,

NannaChar

This book belongs to:

_____

- - - - - - - - - - - - - - - -

_____

Colour us in!

Esse

NannaChar

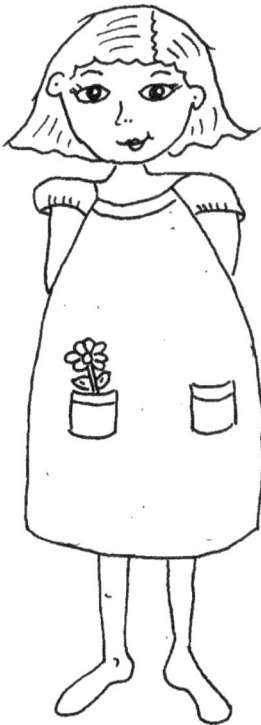

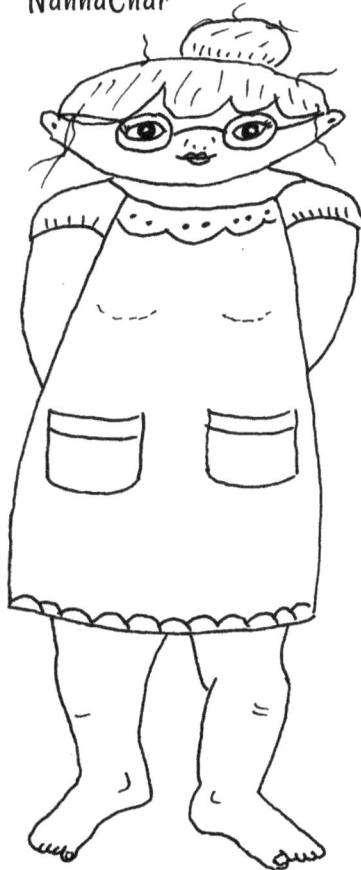

Esse & Friends Learning Books

Hello, I am Annique

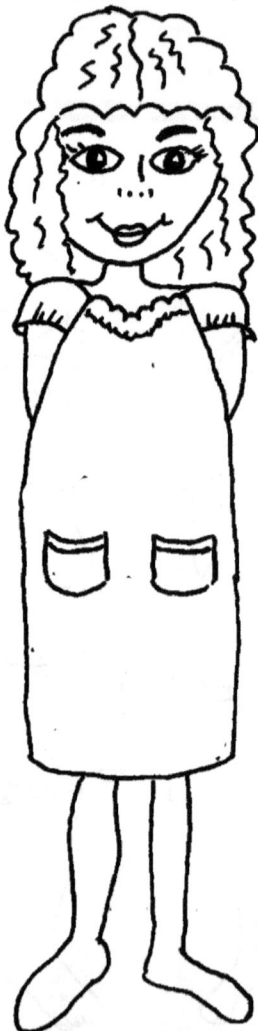

Practice writing this name!

Annique

Hello, I am Bubba

Practice writing this name!

Bubba

Hello, I am
Carolyn

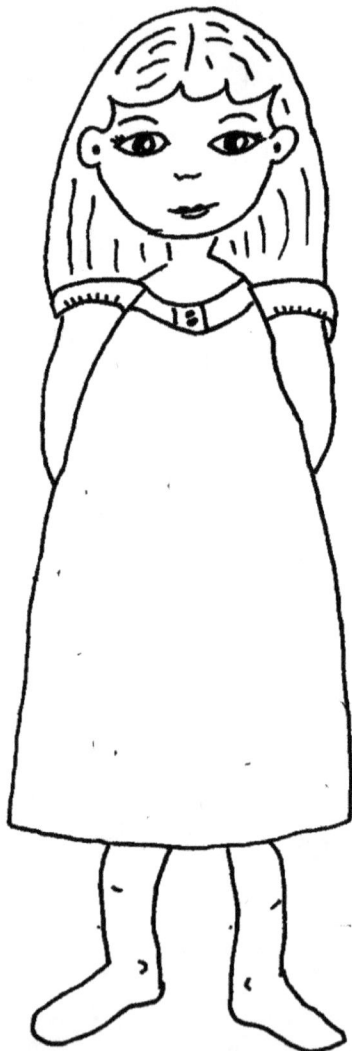

Practice writing this name!

Carolyn

Hello, I am
Danica

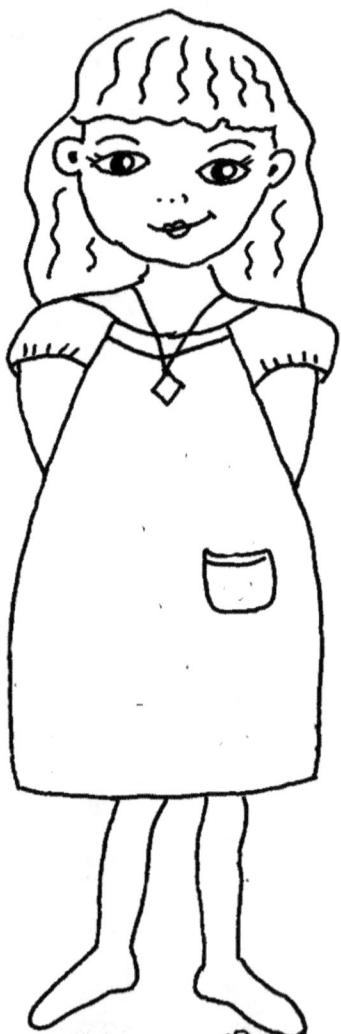

Practice writing this name!

Danica

Hello, I am
Esse

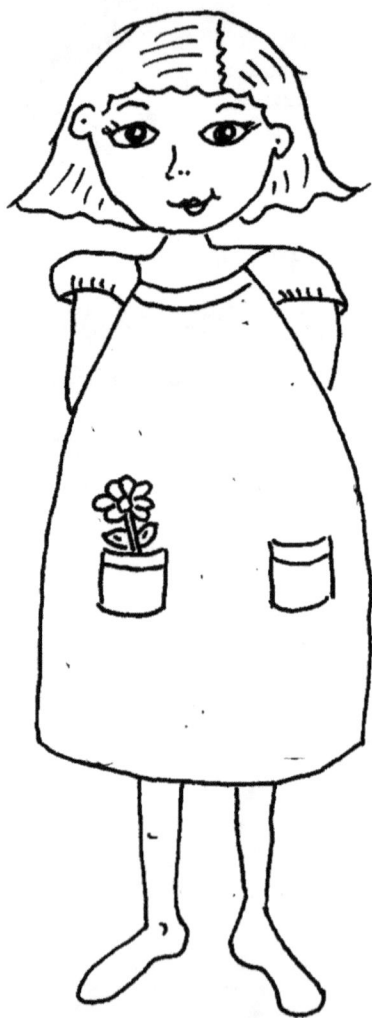

Practice writing this name!

Esse

Hello, I am
Fiona

Practice writing this name!

Fiona

Hello, I am
Gwen

Practice writing this name!

Gwen

Hello, I am
Hermione

Practice writing this name!

Hermione

Hello, I am
Isabella

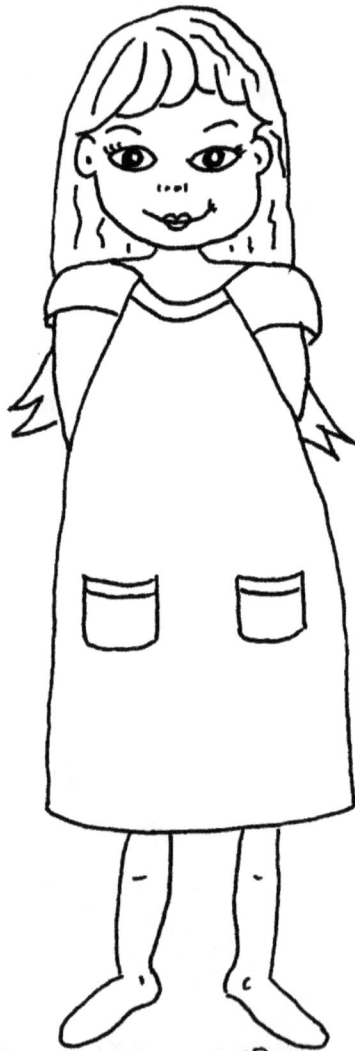

Practice writing this name!

Isabella

Hello, I am
Jessica

Practice writing this name!

Jessica

Hello, I am Kyra

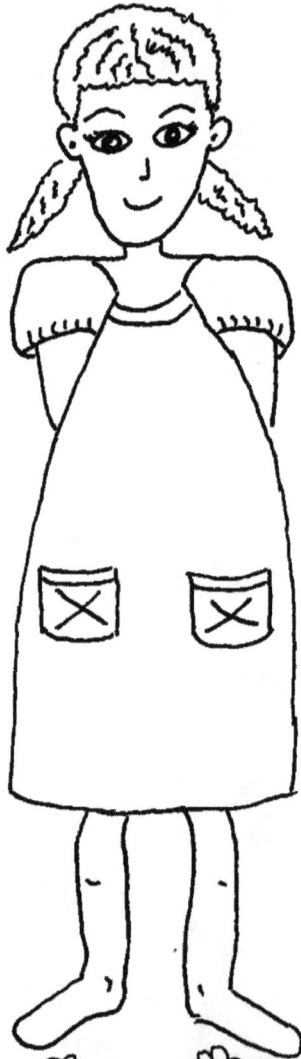

Practice writing this name!

Kyra

Hello, I am
Luna

Practice writing this name!

Luna

Hello, I am Matilda

Practice writing this name!

Matilda

Hello, I am NannaChar

Practice writing this name!

NannaChar

Hello, I am
Olivia

Practice writing this name!

Olivia

Hello, I am Poppy

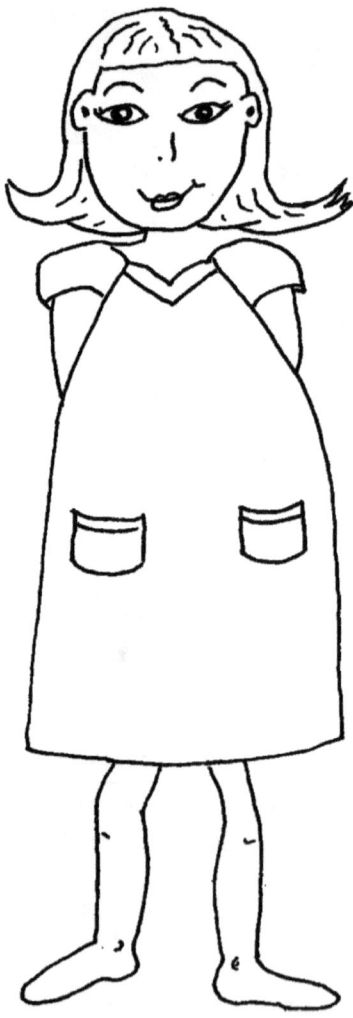

Practice writing this name!

Poppy

Hello, I am
Quin

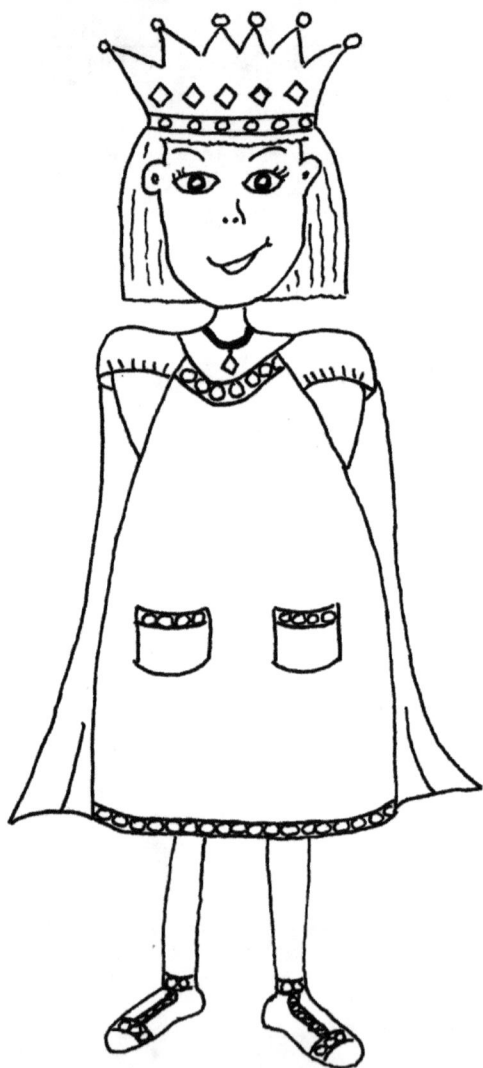

Practice writing this name!

Quin

Hello, I am Rebecca

Practice writing this name!

Rebecca

Hello, I am Sophie

Practice writing this name!

Sophie

Hello, I am
Tahlia

Practice writing this name!

Tahlia

Hello, I am
Ursela

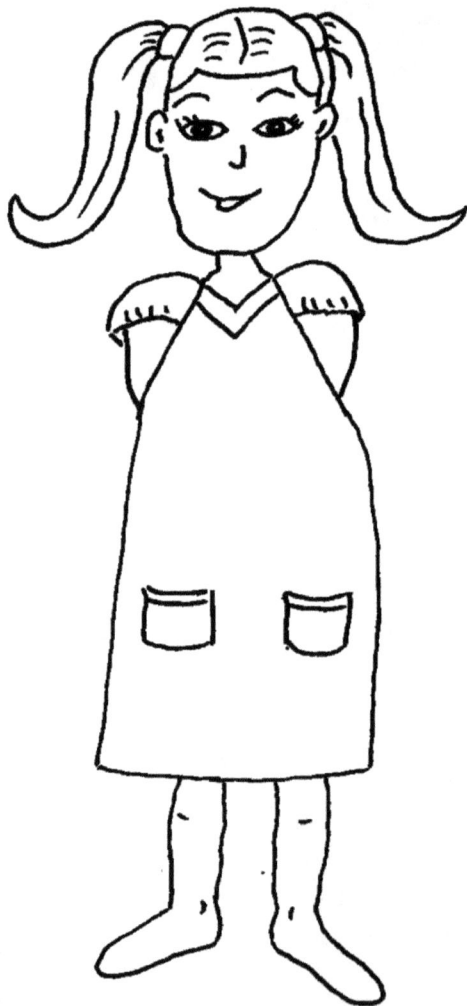

Practice writing this name!

Ursela

Hello, I am Violet

Practice writing this name!

Violet

Hello, I am
Wendy

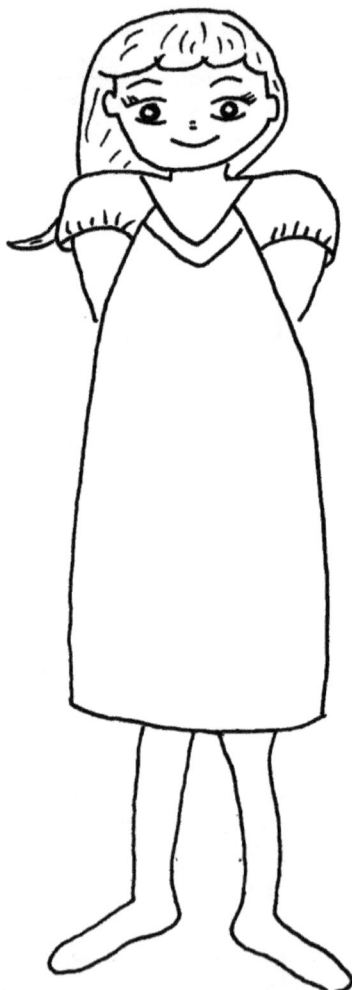

Practice writing this name!

Wendy

Hello, I am
Xuxa

Practice writing this name!

Xuxa

Hello, I am Yvonne

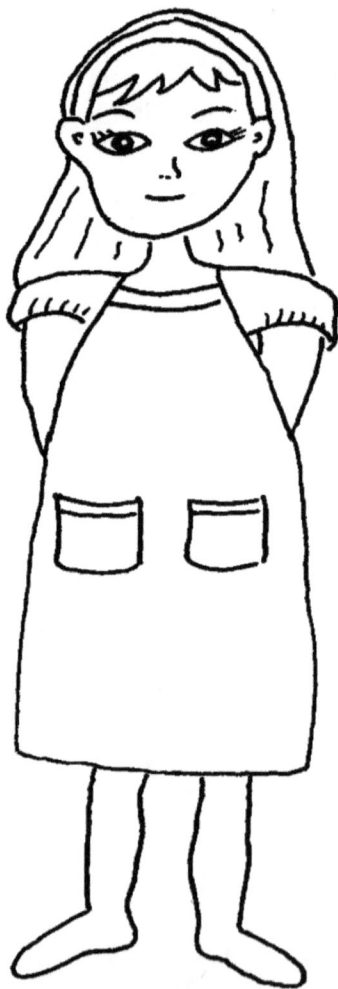

Practice writing this name!

Yvonne

Hello, I am
Zelen

Practice writing this name!

Zeten

MY Name is

_____

Draw a picture of yourself below!

Practice writing this name!

My Friend is

_____

Parents: Write a Family or Friend's Name Above!

Draw a picture of this person below!

Practice writing this name!

My Friend is

_____

Parents: Write a Family or Friend's Name Above!

Draw a picture of this person below!

Practice writing this name!

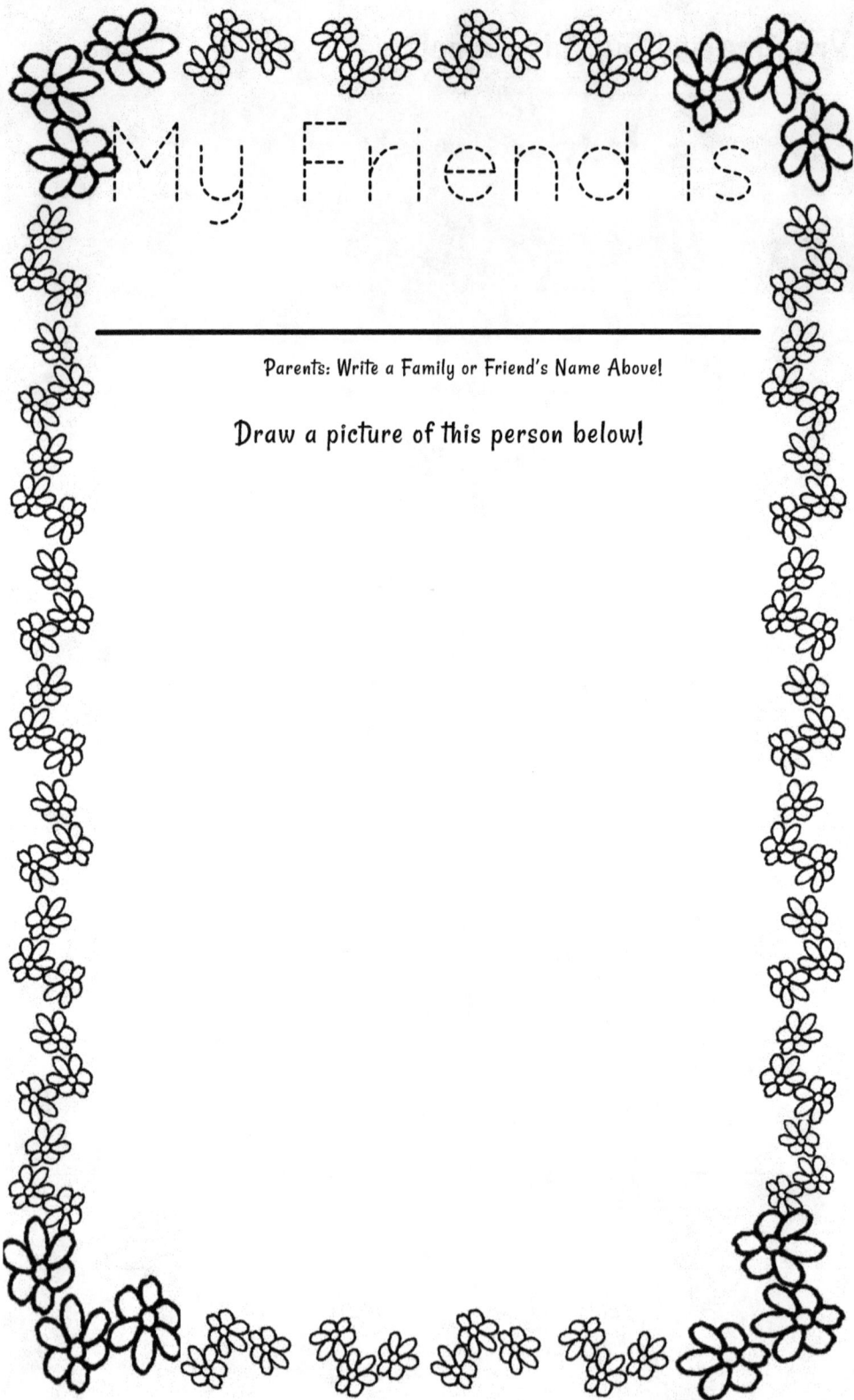

My Friend is

_____

Parents: Write a Family or Friend's Name Above!

Draw a picture of this person below!

Practice writing this name!

My Friend is

_____

Parents: Write a Family or Friend's Name Above!

Draw a picture of this person below!

Practice writing this name!

My Friend is

_____

Parents: Write a Family or Friend's Name Above!

Draw a picture of this person below!

Practice writing this name!

Esse & Friends
Learning Books

Attention Parents and Educators!
You are welcome to contact us to enquire about our
bulk purchasing discounts and discuss our creating
custom words and Esse & Friends interiors.

Be sure to check out the other Colouring and Handwriting
Practice Workbooks in this series. Just look for Esse and
NannaChar on the cover!

www.ingramcontent.com/pod-product-compliance
Lightning Source LLC
Chambersburg PA
CBHW072156020426
42334CB00018B/2031